Training Black Spirit
Ethics for African American Teens

Dr. William L. Conwill

RONIN
Berkeley, CA

"You must never be fearful about
what you are doing when it is right."

—Rosa Parks

Training Black Spirit
Ethics for African American Teens
Dr. William L. Conwill

Training Black Spirit

Copyright: © 2016: William L. Conwill
ISBN: 978-1-57951-222-4

Published by

Ronin Publishing, Inc.

PO Box 3436
Oakland, CA 94609
www.roninpub.com

Production:

    Cover & Book Design: Beverly A. Potter

    Cover image: © Can Stock Photo Inc/Kozzi

    Fonts:

        African, Allen R. Walden

        African Gold, Christopher Kollat, Linotype

        Gurnsey, Fonthead

        Kalimba Family, John Vargas Biltren

        Venis, Chank

Library of Congress Card Number: 2016941113

Printed in the United States   Distributed to the book trade by PGW

"As an artist I come to sing, but as a citizen, I will always speak for peace, and no one can silence me in this."

—Paul Robeson

"The greatest glory in living lies not in never failing, but in rising every time we fail."

—Nelson Mandela

Table of Contents

Foreword 9

Ethics 12

Working With Teens in Groups 19

Adinkra Symbols 23

Ethical Principles & Values as Means of Self-Defense 25

Charisma & Leadership 26

Protect Yourself 28

Nurture Courage 30

Respect Parents 32

Patience 34

Unity in Diversity 36

Wisdom 38

Divine Power 40

Defy Difficulties 42

Abundance 44

Peacemaking 46

Strategy 48

Adaptability 50

Caring 52

Strength & Humility 54

Set Limits 56

Justice 58

Support 60

Table of Contents continued

Independence 62

Circumspection 64

Sharing 66

Serve Others 68

Faith 70

God is Here 72

Hope 74

Infinity of the Soul 76

Trust in God 78

Praise God 80

Intelligence 82

Tenderness 84

Power 86

Faithfulness 88

Persistence 90

Death 92

Readiness 94

Practical Knowledge 96

Improve Yourself 98

Possessiveness 100

Toughness 102

Supportiveness 104

Cooperation 106

Propriety 108

Author Bio 111

foreword

William L. Conwill has a remarkably versatile background in psychology, philosophy, theology, education, martial arts, and fatherhood. This wealth of experience and knowledge makes him more than qualified to offer character-building and consciousness-raising guidelines to teenagers, especially to African American youth who are disproportionately vulnerable to being adversely affected by endemic social injustices and by what progressive, emancipatory theologians call the systemic evils of our society's interlocking inequalities of race, class, and gender.

These evils amount to injurious forms of structural violence—whether blatant or subtle in how they are manifested. According to the late Martin Luther King, Jr.'s social vision, there are three giant evils in the world that should be countered, and to the extent possible, eradicated: racism, poverty, and militarism. These constitute the larger backdrop for the local stage upon which young black men and women can deploy the ethics explained in this insightful handbook.

The guidelines presented in this book represent ethical principles and spiritual values that, if truly comprehended and appropriately applied, can help black youth make their way through the challenges they are likely to face in their passage from childhood and adolescence into full adulthood. The journey toward adulthood is often complicated by various sorts of constraints and obstacles that need to be overcome through effective problem solving and an optimistic sense that there is light at the end of the tunnel.

The wider environmental or societal context in which the journey toward adulthood takes place is ultimately influenced by forces much larger than the interpersonal interactions and conflicts that are the immediate sources of the dilemmas youth must learn to navigate skillfully and responsibly. Navigation across a challenging terrain can be enhanced if informed and guided by principles that have been tried, tested, and adapted for new generations.

Developing principled behaviors and deeper understandings of the world may lead individuals to directions where the application of ethical precepts may have implications for dilemmas at the micro and macro levels. In other words, some of the spiritual values addressed in this engaging text may have relevance beyond the immediate domain of everyday personal and interpersonal dynamics. At moments, the personal is political, ramifying into a more far-ranging field of public interest, power, and social change. To the extent that this happens, ethics and politics converge, becoming complementary dimensions of social action where personal responsibility and collective interests intersect and interplay.

In this book, Dr. Conwill interprets and shows the enduring relevance of ancient principles and values for present-day readers who should encompass adolescents as well as the adults who care about and mentor them. Toward this goal, he elaborates on the spiritual meanings and ethical implications of the key concepts and precepts associated with Ghanaian, specifically Akan, Adinkra symbols.

In his brief and easily digestible explanations, which are coupled with recommended activities, Dr. Conwill encourages youthful readers to become actively involved in thoughtful and thought-provoking exercises that take insights from the text into personal practice and lived experience.

Through this behaviorally or practice-oriented approach, which draws on his expertise in the philosophy and art of self-defense, Dr. Conwill demonstrates the enduring relevance of a West African tradition of wisdom to our lives and those of our children today. He shows how Adinkra concepts can influence the ways young people defend themselves against and move forward in their life journey in spite of the prevalence of destructive influences in the world.

Black youth can benefit from ethical and spiritual training to prepare themselves for the complexities and contradictions that characterize today's society and world. Our society gives higher priority to building prisons than schools. A 2008 Pew Center report predicted that if current trends in racial profiling and institutionalized racism in the criminal justice system continue, we can expect to see as much as a third of the black male population incarcerated in the future. Moreover, the incarceration rate for black women is also rising, so the problem is not only one that targets males.

On the more positive side, there are trends that promote the reintegration and revitalization of black community life, assigning youth to constructive roles rather than assuming their inevitable descent into delinquency and troublemaking. Besides the successful school programs that receive very little attention in the media, there are extracurricular and community-based projects employing hip-hop-inflected pedagogies for mobilizing youth toward community- building outcomes.

Dr. Conwill seeks to achieve the objective of communal revitalization through a different means. He translates and encodes Adinkra precepts into black youth's everyday practical consciousness. His project situates ethics for black youth within a historical context in which the relevance of African cultural heritage persists in African American identity and well-being.

Training Black Spirit deserves to be widely read and discussed in homes, schools, community centers, churches, and other community venues, such as barbershops and other settings where grassroots philosophers assemble to reason and rap. I recommend the book as well as its author, who is available for speaking engagements, group encounters, and training sessions related to rites of passage and leadership development among youth. His extensive expertise, knowledge, and wisdom make him an exemplary role model and educator.

—Faye V. Harrison, Ph.D.
President
International Union of Anthropological
and Ethnological Sciences

Ethics

Ethics is a system of moral conduct, that is, a set of principles by which we live. These principles are accepted rules about how people should carry themselves. Over time, different cultures, depending on what they consider to be the nature of the human person, produce different sets of moral philosophies—ethics—for guidance. For example, during those eras when men and women were considered sinners primarily, penitential living and the search for forgiveness and salvation were their major preoccupations.

In the twentieth century, however, after the Freudian revolution, the prevailing notion within educated circles was that neurotic men and women were characterized by their struggle to keep their sexual desires under control through repression. As a result, many sought economic prosperity and to practice sexuality free from guilt.

Many young people are confused about what they should or should not be doing and how they should act toward each other. They are searching. "Is it okay to call people certain names referring to race?" "I like to keep it real. Why should I talk all proper?" "Should I follow my family's expectations or do what I want with my life?" "Why should I care whether my parents don't like my style of clothes?" "What's so wrong about using drugs if everybody does it?"

Hip-hop offers direction to some. Mega-church televangelists offer guidance to others. Icons like Bill Cosby and Russell Simmons also like to give advice. Who is right?

Globalization and Ethical Confusion

Much of the uncertainty and confusion we see today is related to globalization. In globalization, the business practices of very large and powerful multinational corporations increasingly break down local processes of communication, trade, and ownership, and they direct the flow of money to themselves instead of those who help produce their wealth. The world at large is their marketplace.

Globalization makes you feel like what's going on around on the other side of the world is just as important as what's going on in your own neighborhood. Increasingly, in response to the confusion that comes from the feeling that everything everywhere is important, we are told we must accept a "diversity" of viewpoints about what is wrong or right, with questions like "Can't we all just get along?"

Sometimes we can, and sometimes we won't. Bombings, wars, and mass shootings are signals that we don't. When an individual or a group decides to "take it to the streets," it's a sign that some people no longer feel like arguing whether or not their point of view is the most valid or important. Where and when do we take a stand?

People stand on principles all the time. Many are willing to die for their principles. They feel it's important to live out their ethics, to live out what they believe in. It's important, therefore, to be aware and selective about the principles by which we are willing to live or die.

Ethics for African American Teens

The particular set of ethical principles that we practice reflects those values that we have decided to follow, in order to preserve our way of life. Cultures take their time in laying out their values clearly. People outside a given culture can't always relate to what goes on inside it.

When we sometimes say to people who have not grown up in a particular culture, "You wouldn't understand," we really mean it. We don't expect them to understand. For example, when Alice Walker campaigned against female genital mutilation in some African cultures, a lot of African women told her that she should go back to her own country and talk to people in her own American community about their own sexuality, and that she didn't understand that of African women. Those cultures had their own values regarding sexuality, and they wanted to be given their proper respect. Practices that we might consider cruel or barbaric or archaic at the beginning of the third millennium might well be central to their ways of life. Cultures take care of a people's sense of identity, and they preserve a community's viability or prospects of continuity. Break the rules—break the culture.

African American cultural communities are no different. Black cultural traditions stress our essence as embodied, intelligent spiritual beings who express ourselves in the spiritual, cognitive, emotional, and behavioral spheres of human experience. Ethics for black teens should promote the healthy development of the black person as a member of the family, the community, and the world.

The rules of behavior that governed black people traditionally when local area processes such as enslavement and unemployment tested our humanity preserved our culture and made our survival possible. These rules have come under assault increasingly from macro-processes like urbanization and globalization. During our transitions from plantations to tenant farms to housing projects to suburbs, we have also moved from one room schoolhouses to segregated city schools to integrated academies. We've moved from country prayer arbors to large churches and mosques to being "too fly" for God.

It's easy to get lost in the confusion. Look at all the young black boys who are thrown out of school because of belligerence when they are "dissed" by teachers, young black teen girls in love who become disillusioned and pregnant after succumbing to the seduction of older men, young black gangbangers who thought that by killing, they would gain respect and grab the mantle of adulthood, and young black ex-prisoners who search sadly for a world where they really can be winners.

What sort of life will any black youth have without a personal and conscious examination of the principles that have allowed us to survive, and that have produced some of the richest, most creative gifts to our nation and world? What else besides the gift of a book on ethics for black teens could be more appropriate for training them to take a meaningful role in society and the world?

Training Black Spirit

The principles presented this book come from working with incarcerated young people, college students, hospital patients, families of single black mothers, and families that fostered or adopted African American children. Many were at high-risk for becoming severely impaired adults. Things had happened to them that were very likely to affect their development in a very negative way.

Why I Do What I Do

I am a healer. The ideas I talk about in this book come mainly from working with incarcerated young people, with college students, with hospital patients, with families of single Black mothers, and with families that fostered or had adopted African American children. Many of those who came to see me were adolescents whose parents were drug- and alcohol-addicted, or children who had witnessed extremely violent acts in their homes, or children who had suffered intense and prolonged sexual abuse as infants or toddlers. In all these settings, I constantly found myself "breaking it down" so that the concepts were easy to understand. I enjoyed this aspect of my practice at first. It made me feel smart, something psychologists aren't supposed to admit! People were vibing strongly to my ideas about how we should decide what to do under various conditions, and telling me they liked this approach.

As a psychologist and a healer, I learned to use powerful methods for influencing behavior. I was very aware of the need to be respectful of the rights of my clients to determine their own objectives, particularly in therapy. Telling people what they should do by telling them how to think about a problem, no matter how "directive" or "nondirective" my therapy with a particular client was, seemed a risky business to me. For years, I was uneasy with the notion that I was teaching ethics under the guise of therapy.

As I began working with more and more seriously emotionally and physically ill people, I discovered that their own ethical frameworks, oftentimes unclear or implicit, were often part of the problem! Making their present mode of ethical decision-making and its behavioral expressions explicit and reflexively discussing alternatives made me feel safer, and it helped those who came to see me! In fact, many—given the missing bit of ethical background information needed for generating the "correct" solution to their problems—seemed to get better almost instantly. People were coming to me for advice on how to think about their problems rather than simply asking me to help them get rid of them. However, I still felt a nagging pull.

I didn't feel like I was anybody's role model, and I sure wasn't going to start living my life according to anyone else's expectations if I could help it. What gave me the right to tell others what I thought they should do? I knew that many of the answers came to me easily, having been trained to recognize various types of questions as a philosophy student in college. What were the rules for telling others what I thought they should do?

Is the right thing to do the same for everybody? No. That's the reason we need ethics for black teens.

Psychologists used to operate as though we developed impartial clinical insight as a result of our training and that our scientifically based treatment kept our own values out of therapy. Twenty-five years ago, this was easier to believe, if we were middle-class, American, white males who worked only with others like ourselves. However, in response to societal changes about forty years ago, psychology training programs began accepting more ethnic minorities and more women.

Now, psychologists don't feel as smug about challenges to their own unexamined ethnic and gender biases. Being aware of ethical issues when working across lines of ethnicity as well as gender and sexuality has become more of a standard of expected practice as psychologists have become more honest about the nature of the therapy. Some psychologists have related their uneasiness with ethical questions in therapy to an ethos of near-narcissism, with self-fulfillment and expressive individualism as goals rather than family and community responsibility.

As more and more academic and practicing psychologists accepted the fact that white American middle-class standards and modes of interaction were not necessarily right standards and modes of interaction with clients who were ethnically different from themselves, we began the slow and often painful process of expanding psychologists' awareness and knowledge base.

Black, Asian, Latino, and Native American perspectives were developed for the purpose of training American practitioners and researchers to work with people who were not white, not male, not native-born, and not English-speaking. Feminist, gay, lesbian, and bisexual perspectives soon followed suit. Restructuring the curriculum and practice of psychologists is a tedious, and sometimes painful process. I am still involved in this work of changing the profession.

Traditional Wisdom

Training Black Spirit is written in the aphoristic style of traditional wisdom literature. That means it uses lots of short maxims, proverbs, and adages, or short sayings about life that many people consider to be true, to state or comment on personal standards of conduct. You may not understand some things clearly at first, and you may need to ask an adult you trust to help you with it. Give things time to sink in. *Training Black Spirit* challenges you to figure out what's important, determine where your values lie, and become more united in head—how you see things—and heart—what moves you—and hand—how you respond to the demands of your situation. It's your personal trainer in the area of ethics, or directions on proper living. Although I use the word "God" several times in this book, you may substitute other names denoted for the Author of the universe, depending on your religious beliefs.

The principles in *Training Black Spirit* are based on traditional African values. They should be interpreted as directives or instructions by which to live as well as means of self-defense against destructive influences.

The principles are represented by Adinkra symbols. A self-defense interpretation for each of the principles is written after an Adinkra symbol. On the facing page, there is a meditative reading to help you gain insight into the principle. The Adinkra symbol helps you learn to focus quickly on the principle when necessary. Eventually, an ability to reflect on the principle will become habitual with the viewing of the symbol. The concepts behind *Training Black Spirit* draw on brain science, transpersonal psychology, mainstream psychiatry, and ancient traditions.

This brief synopsis, as well as the book, is abstract, just as a simple line drawing of a person is abstract, meaning it points out just the skeletal elements of the ideas. You have to interact with the text, think things out, and figure out what it means for you.

You can interact with the text by getting together with friends and talking about a particular question, or about one of the ideas you found challenging, or hard to go along with. Sometimes you may discover ways to think about a particular topic that you had not considered before.

"In the end we will
remember not the words of
our enemies, but the silence
of our friends."

—Martin Luther King, Jr.

Working with Teens in Groups

As a psychologist and consultant, I frequently worked with more than three or four people at a time. For example, when I worked with juvenile delinquents, there were anywhere from 30-45 fellows at a time in my unit receiving group guidance that routinely led to decreased violence during my shifts. As a college counselor, I left my door open for people to "drop in and relax" unless a particular student had made an appointment for an individual session at that time. Other psychologists tended to keep their doors closed all the time, and thought it strange that I often had a room-full of students talking about college social and organizational issues in my office, while their contact was limited to individual sessions with only a handful of students a day.

When I directed a clinic at a university hospital for people who were suffering from long-term pain disorders and stress, I treated most of my patients in groups rather than individually. As Chief Psychologist for a Children & Youth Division of a State Psychiatric Institute, I started out the young children's day with a group session in the classroom. Most had received diagnoses of Attention Deficit Disorder and Oppositional Defiant Disorder. Before I arrived at the Institute, the children were placed routinely on medications for several months before they demonstrated improvement. I used group therapy in the classroom at the start of their school day to make their adjustment to the hospital easier. I used drumming, chanting, calming rituals, and social skill training and practice, so that within a week, the children learned to trust each other to self-correct if they had hurt someone's feelings. I have made presentations at medical conferences on the use of ritual in therapeutic sessions to explain what I was doing.

My experience working in groups goes back to the late 1960s, when intensive sensitivity training was seen as a way to help people change their attitudes quickly. By the early 1970s, I had been influenced in graduate school by one of the most respected experts on group therapy theory, and begun conducting group therapy in a university institute. By the 1980s, I had advanced practitioner of group therapy certificates on my office wall. I wrote and co-wrote articles on using group approaches, as I worked with colleagues from the Journal for Specialists in Group Work. All this to say, from my perspective, working with groups of teens makes sense, and so I recommend group work for those who want to use this book to help Black teens develop. Here are some helpful hints.

Simple Group Themes

Merely getting teens together to talk can generate a lot of anxiety in a group. In the first few sessions, a lot of things have to happen. The teens have to learn what the group is all about: its goals, its objectives, its rules. They have to learn to trust the group leaders. They have to learn to discuss ideas courageously, and disagree without insulting others or putting them down, and find common ground in talking about the values they believe in.

It's hard to get a group of teens together without getting a clown or two. Clowns let you know their identity quite quickly. This is also true for a group of people who are older than teenagers! Don't worry about checking the clowns. The teens in the group will help keep them in line if they see the need. On the flip side, clowns create a lot of energy in the group. They bring humor. They bring insight. They ask questions that take the conversations to new levels. They're like comics; they can be relied upon to say what the problem is when everyone else keeps silent. Don't keep them out of your group. Bring in the clowns.

When teens discuss certain topics, like sexuality and male-female relationship issues especially, they don't like to open themselves to criticism or disapproval from authority figures. So it's important to maintain group confidentiality. Make sure the teens obtain parental consent before they join the group. Have the teens sign an agreement that what gets said in the group stays in the group and an understanding that they will respect each other's right to safety in the group. No insults, no threats, no rudeness, and so forth. I always give teens a chance to make up the rules, so that they are invested in maintaining limits of proper composure. Those who are not members of the group, therefore, should not be present. So don't bring in passers-by, parents, siblings, friends, spectators, pets, auditors, or others.

Each member of the group should have their own copy of *Training Black Spirit*, which has lots of topics involving ethics. Some topics are concerned with personal intellectual, physical and spiritual development. Others are related to family and friendship relationships, while others encourage the development of citizenship. If you plan to work with your teen group over several sessions, you might cover a couple of similar topics in each meeting. Give reading assignments at the end of each session, with someone from the group calling members to check off if they have finished the reading. This is a way of developing leadership and building camaraderie within the group.

Develop opening and closing rituals for your group. For example, if one of the group leaders is an elder, you may have that person call the group to order each session, and to ask the teens to focus their attention and energy onto the group's objectives, and onto the needs of the those in the group. Another ritual teens enjoy is for the group to sing a particular song at the beginning and/or end of the meetings. As part of the opening ritual, it is important that group leaders begin each session with a recount of the objectives and the purpose of the meeting.

Depending on the size of the group, you may want to divide the group into sections so that everyone gets to contribute to small-group discussions. The larger the "small-group", the more likely that a few participants will dominate the exchanges. It is important that everyone in the group feel included.

While we're talking about size of the group, let me tell you what I sometimes do when I have a lot of people in front of me. Let's say I have 50 participants. I have them count off by fours in order. All those who said "One" go to the left back corner of the room; the "Twos" go to the rear right corner; the "Threes" move to the front right corner, and so forth. This makes the groups' size pretty equal, and also splits up people who came in together. Assign someone in each group to write down the main points they discussed in order to make a report to the large group.

Don't be in a hurry, because the teens will pick that up and react. Spend five minutes with the opening, take a couple of minutes to get into groups, or a circle. Discussion for 20 minutes. Take 10 minutes for Reflections and Wrap-up. Use a minute to assign a topic for the next session, and perform your closing ritual. Take your time, but end each session at the allotted time. After a few sessions, you will see a rhythm evolving. I hope these pointers help you structure your Training Black Spirit discussion sessions. Relax and trust the process!

"If you wanna fly, you got to give up the shit that weighs you down."

— Chloe Ardelia Wofford
aka Toni Morrison

Adinkra Symbols

Adinkra symbols are stylized pictures that represent the philosophy and culture of the Asante (Akan) people of Ghana. They symbolize beliefs, cultural and personal values, social and political organizations, and can stand for proverbs, maxims, and wise sayings.

The pictures can be of people and the objects they use, plants, animals, parts of the human body, designs in nature, and abstract ideas such as love, caring, and unity. In Ghana, these symbols can be found on cloth to signify the respect for the attributes of a loved one who has passed. The symbols may be used to communicate with the dead, who, the Asante believe, act as mediators between God and the people.

Origins of the Symbols

There is more than one theory on the origins of the Adinkra symbols, but I will focus on the one developed by the spiritual Akan. Okomfo Anokye, the first chief priest of the Asante, according to legend, conjured the Golden Stool from the heavens, to seat the soul of the king. The Golden Stool represents the power

Sankofa: it is not taboo to return to fetch something that has been forgotten.

*Adinkra symbols recorded
by Robert Sutherland Rattray, 1927*

invested in the first king, or Asantehena, Osei Tutu, as well as his successors.

Stools are common in African ritual, and in African-inspired art performances. The Golden Stool represents the soul of the Asante, living, dead and yet to be born. According to legend, when the Golden Stool came down to the people, it was covered with a cloth with Adinkra symbols. This theory suggests that the symbols have been in use for 1500 years or so.

Adinkra symbols have names in Twi, the language of the Asante. "Sankofa", for example, is the Twi name for the symbol representing the wise saying that it is not taboo to return to fetch something that has been forgotten. In other words, it is important to remember one's history.

One version of Sankofa looks somewhat like a heart, but it represents two birds looking backwards, with their front facing forward. Another version of Sankofa is more clearly a bird looking backwards with a gourd in its mouth.

Children learn the meaning of the various symbols over time and reflect on the wisdom of their people as they grow up. Adinkra symbols can be seen on buildings, art, clothes, tattoos, and jewelry in African American communities in the US. If you are paying attention, the symbols can tell a lot about the spirit of the person or object displaying it.

Ethical Principles & Values as Means of Self-Defense

George Washington Carver

Rules for Teens to Live by

1. Be clean both inside and out;
2. Neither look up to the rich nor down to the poor;
3. Lose, if need be, without squealing;
4. Win without bragging;
5. Always be considerate of women, children and older people;
6. Be too brave to lie;
7. Be too generous to cheat;
8. Take your share of the world and let others take theirs.

CHARISMA & LEADERSHIP
Be the leader you would follow.

I asked one of my sons when he was in the 4th grade, "Do you have a hero?" Of course, I thought for sure he'd say, "You, papa." Instead, he thought for a couple of seconds, and named off his favorite rap artist. I had to eat a big slice of humble pie. We all want to be a hero, someone everybody looks up to as a great leader. We all want to be great leaders, even if it's to help someone else be great leaders. What do great leaders look like? Great leaders have learned to apply themselves in a strong way to do something positive for many people. They have used their talents and their desire to dedicate themselves to achieve a goal.

Some leaders have household names, names we have all heard growing up. For example, Isabella Baumfree, better known as Sojourner Truth, was born in slavery in New York about 1797, and sold to at least four owners before escaping in 1826. She worked for many years to make slavery in America against the law. She advocated for women's equality with men. She traveled the country speaking about human rights. She is a hero.

> ## Suggested Activity
> **Each day, do one thing that uses your talents to help others.**

Percy Julian is another. He was born in Birmingham, Alabama in 1899. He was a brilliant scientist, a chemist, who eventually won international respect for his work in the development of hormones and of compounds for the treatment of eye disorders, rheumatoid arthritis, and other diseases. When he died in Chicago in 1975, he was known as a great chemist all around the world.

My late friend, Jim Haskins, was an outstanding author who wrote books on great African Americans for young people. When I first met Jim, I had found his book on Ragtime composer Scott Joplin in a used books store. Ragtime was a music style at the start of the 20th century that stressed a raggedy rhythm. I bought the book, and brought it home for my children to read. I admired Jim as someone who had followed his passion, doing what he really enjoyed doing for others, and it had made him great. We find greatness in people who love what they do for others. We have many models of great leadership, and we admire them. We celebrate their lives. We want to be like them. They inspire us. We talk about them with respect. We tell stories about their lives. We create plays about them. We read books about them. We dress like they do. We imitate them.

ADINKRAHENE

"Chief of the Adinkra symbols"

Recognize greatness within you.

Greatness & Leadership

Be the leader you are waiting for.

PROTECT YOURSELF
Be a survivor.

Protecting ourselves from harm is instinctual. By paying attention to the consequences of our actions, we can learn what leads to harm, from simple colds to severe injury. Once we learn what harms us, we should have little confusion about whether to avoid the harmful condition. For example, cooling too quickly after opening our pores through profuse sweating, exposing ourselves to viruses, or laying ourselves open to strong-arm robbery are conditions we should regularly avoid whenever possible, without too much training.

Suggested Activity

Examine the ways in which you protect yourself from bad things happening to you.

Sometimes we see examples of sensible people not acting in self-defense, but this usually is attributable to altruism: medical scientists testing vaccines on themselves, firemen saving people from burning buildings, or living organ donors.

When we see people not protecting themselves from harm for no sensible reason, we should suspect some sort of illness that should be treated. Failing that, we should begin to wonder about extremely low self-esteem.

In the study of the martial art of karate, instructors teach students to defend themselves by moving away from or blocking punches and kicks and strikes. Students learn how to protect certain body parts such as the head and chest that if hit, might hurt them severely. They learn techniques to block powerful kicks that might kill them. They also learn to counter, to deliver an offensive technique of their own. Eventually, the student masters the impulse to react with alarm when he is under attack, and learns to counter more and more quickly and effectively. Eventually, the counter becomes more or less immediate. At the higher end of the practice of defense, some funny things start to happen. The student learns to "feel" when his opponent is about to attack, and beats him to the punch. After years of practice in the art of self-defense, he can learn to prevent people from even wanting to attack him.

"War Horn"

A horn sounds the battle cry.

Vigilance & Wariness

Recognize dangers.

NURTURE COURAGE
Be strong in the face of fear.

You are called upon to be a hero. It doesn't matter who you are, how rich you are, how protected you feel, or how much leadership training you have. The tests of your Courage, Valor, and Heroism are going to come in the form of standing up to a bully at school, protesting for social justice, or rescuing people from a burning building.

For some, the tests come early and often. For others, there may be fewer tests. The early tests might present themselves in the form of a neighborhood or a classroom bully that asks for your lunch money. You pass the test if you report to an adult who is in charge. As you grow, you may fear your friends' ridicule when you volunteer to answer a teacher's question. You pass the test when you stand up and answer anyway. You may fear your classmates' laughter if you spell a word incorrectly during a Spelling Bee. You pass the test when you sign up for the Spelling Bee anyway. By the time you are a teen-ager, you may be tempted to sit quietly and keep your hands down to keep from being embarrassed at school. You pass the test when you participate and speak up in the class anyway. You may have become too afraid to disagree with people who express hateful attitudes or who intimidate helpless people. You pass the test when you tell them that their attitude is wrong. You intervene when you see someone mistreating others. You correct people who treat us disrespectfully. You are willing to step up and speak out.

Suggested Activity

Find a quiet place where you can meditate. It might be your church or your bedroom. Spend time there each day thinking of how you handled your fears.

Heroes overcome their fears of being laughed at, of feeling small, of looking stupid, and even of dying. You nurture your Courage, Valor and Heroism every day when you recognize opportunities to speak up or do something when you see things are amiss, and you act on that recognition. "If you see something, say something" is not a saying aimed only at certain people. It's for everybody.

AKOFENA

"Sword of war "

The crossed swords are a shield.

Courage, Valor, & Heroism

Courage and valor are shields.

RESPECT PARENTS
Good parenting takes setting loving limits.

Your parents took on a serious social role when they decided to give you life. In African American communities, good parenting has always included the notion that the main function of the Black family is to rear children. In general, the minimal requirements for parents are to provide nourishment, protection, and supervision for their children. By the time your parents are no longer legally responsible for your care, you should be capable of some level of self-support.

Teaching discipline is one of the main tasks of parents in the education of their children. Discipline can be described as learning to follow rules and standards in one's behavior. Parents are legally obliged to keep their minor (under legal age of adulthood) children from certain acts, such as truancy or skipping school, staying out too late without supervision or breaking curfew, drinking liquor, and other behavior that may be detrimental to their health. Parents who fail to enforce discipline can be fined and forced to perform community service. Conversely, by law, children must obey their parents.

> ## Suggested Activity
> **Write a list of the skills you've acquired as a result of following your parents' rules.**

The ideal of teaching discipline with love and mercy comes as a divine gift. Teaching discipline with love means that the parent builds a relationship in which the child can feel cherished and wanted and warm. Teaching discipline with mercy means letting the child know that no matter what, the parent will forgive the child when the child does wrong.

This means that when teens fail to meet their parents' expectations, parents should not reject them or tell them that they are no longer loved. If a teen is thrown into situations that are too challenging because of inadequate preparation, and fails, they should not be made to feel that their parents no longer accept them as members of the family, no matter what. Whether you like your parents or not, you should have respect for their roles, because it allows you a clearheaded understanding of their and your responsibilities. Regard your parents respectfully.

AKOKO NAN

"The leg of a hen"

The hen treads on her chicks, but does not kill them.

Nurturing & Discipline

Nurture children, but do not pamper them.

PATIENCE
Keep an even temperment to gain understanding.

Patient people are warm, humble, generous, forgiving and peaceful, while hotheads curse and blow their top when things don't go their way. They are thrown off-balance by demands. Their explosive tempers create turmoil as they make a mess of things by disturbing everyone.

People who holler at others to hurry up are impatient. People who jump in front of the line are impatient. Someone will have to jump in and straighten them out if they don't learn to control themselves better. They have to learn to tolerate change!

Patience contains an element of suffering that we have to learn to tolerate. Becoming patient means learning to tolerate, or put up with your uncomfortable feelings instead of becoming upset and hollering and making a spectacle of yourself. It is this tolerance that brings you to a higher level of wisdom and understanding.

> ## Suggested Activity
>
> **Place a pan of cold water on a stove. Adjust the heat to low. Keep your eyes on the pot, stopping only to blink. Stare at the pot until the water boils. "A watched pot never boils" is not simply an adage.**

That wisdom makes a better person out of you, eventually turning you into a person who knows how to treat others more kindly. Usually we think of patience as waiting for something we want to happen, but this view is only partly correct. The waiting has to be active. It's not enough to mark time by pacing while you wait, like a tiger at the zoo around feeding time who can't go out and catch his food.

You have to learn to attend to a process while you wait. Like a wise obstetrician who attends a child's birth, you must learn to trust the long process, staying calm and attentive as you simply monitor the moans—and holding off the nurses who constantly mumble something about inducing labor so they can all go home. Watching a mother's joy after her hard labor to bring forth her child and witnessing her strong, confident bonding right after she gives birth are the rewards of patience. Take your time. Be patient.

AKOMA

"The heart"

The tolerant person is said to have a heart in his stomach.

Patience & Tolerance

Accept others as they are.

UNITY IN DIVERSITY
You don't have to be a copy-cat to be in solidarity with others.

The spirit of the principle of Understanding and Agreement, Akoma Ntoso—linked hearts—challenges you to build community in a society that serves all us. This notion of linked hearts binds us together generally as equals. You have a part to play in your community every day.

About 100 years ago, the Harlem area of New York City became a place where Black peoples, sometimes referred to as "the New Negroes," from various Caribbean and South American countries and the United States explored the possibilities that the New World of the Americas held for them. The Black scholars and artists of the Harlem Renaissance self-consciously nurtured their own cultural forms of literature, painting, sculpture, and music in response to the differences in their experiences. Their explosive burst of creativity and insight found expression throughout several decades in murals in public buildings, in music, cultural critiques, plays, novels, poetry and other arts. Their names include Langston Hughes, Claude McKay, Zora Neale Hurston, Richard Wright, Duke Ellington, Billie Holiday, and Bessie Smith.

> ## Suggested Activity
> Draw up a list of the roles needed in your community to assure community functions. How do these roles fit together?

We refer to this cultural re-awakening as the "Harlem Renaissance". Much like today's hip-hop movement, it refers to a time when many people became aware of the richness of the Black experience, despite the belief of many Americans that Black people could not produce anything worth their attention.

For over a hundred years, many scholars have studied the Harlem Renaissance era. They meet regularly to agree on ideas that are still applicable today, so that we do not lose touch with our authenticity, and who we are. Hip-hop artists and scholars today, for example, use many ideas from the Harlem Renaissance. They insist that everyone, including the people many would not think of as important, has the individual potential to create tremendous value in his or her community. We are all different with diverse talents and skills. We don't all do the same thing. Everyone's part is important. Find your part, and play it.

AKOMA NTOSO

"Linked hearts"

We each play a part in reaching the goal.

Understanding & Agreement

Work with others.

WISDOM
Look for the "Big Picture".

The ancients prayed incessantly for their leaders to have wisdom so the people would not be led needlessly into slaughter, famine, poverty, or slavery. The wise leader prayed at the throne of Wisdom, usually depicted as a bountiful goddess. Today, each one of us—not just the king or the emperor—needs to seek wisdom and its fruits. This requires looking beyond what is immediately apparent or gratifying—being able to see the big picture.

Seeing the big picture requires a mature style of decision making based on experience. For this reason, many people we consider wise leaders tend to have much exposure to the prevailing conditions, and are often older than their followers.

Suggested Activity

Study the steps wise leaders like Thurgood Marshall and Mary McLeod Bethune took as they planned momentous changes that affected our nation.

Developing your leadership skills daily with the principle of wisdom means living consciously with the great philosophical questions of the past, with crises, and with their resolutions. These questions include "What is right? What is wrong?" "What is the nature of the human being?" "How can I live wisely?"

The principle of Ananse Ntontan, wisdom and creativity, implies that we should not hoard what we know in an effort to keep others powerless and unhealthy. The expression "Knowledge is power" is expressed frequently among those who understand that keeping people in ignorance allows the powerful to take advantage of them. Unfortunately, we live in a society that tends to reward those who exploit people's ignorance at many levels. Examples in our society include using tricky language to describe new laws for voters, misrepresenting facts in news reports to cover up wrong-doing, and charging exorbitant prices for necessary medicines to generate huge profits for shareholders.

Wise leaders should act on behalf of the people. When each of us has taken individual responsibility to act as a wise leader, our collective wisdom will make it difficult for tricksters to manipulate us into accepting oppressive conditions as if they benefit us.

ANANSE NTONTAN

"Spider's web"

No one has all the wisdom in the world.

Wisdom & Creativity

Respect the wisdom of those who show you the way.

DIVINE POWER
Keep a peaceful mind and the Lord will guide you.

The principle of Providence is associated with what is referred to as the theological virtue of hope, which allows us the emotional drive to "keep on keeping on." To practice hope by living according to the principle of Providence is to be in "be at the right place at the right time." Worrying about whether we will be able to cope with what lies ahead can be destructive if we allow it. Dr. Beverly Potter, a nationally respected inspirational management consultant, starts off her book, *The Worrywart's Companion* with a citation from John Milton: "The mind is its own place, and in itself can make a heaven of hell, a hell of heaven."

Suggested Activity

Figure out how you learned to worry. Break the habit of worrying. Resolve to stop wasting precious moments of your life.

My friend, the late Dr. Virginia A. Price, was a therapist. Her Northern California practice was largely with people who were recovering from heart attacks. She frequently advised her anxious patients to "remember we live in a benevolent universe." Like the soothing voice of a best friend, this mantra was useful for keeping them grounded when they worried too much about the future.

Often, we observe people close to death have torturous worries about their lives. They fear they have not measured up to the moral standards of a good life. They worry that others find them lacking. They do not look forward to the aftermath of such a reckoning, especially if they have been raised on a diet of guilt, shame, disdain and contempt. There are true failings and there are inauthentic failings. In our last days, acting with the principle of Providence requires an acknowledgment of our true failings, like our refusal to apologize to those we have hurt purposefully, rather than those attributed to us by those driven by their own desire to condemn us, and appropriate action on our part. Providence uses honesty, at any time of our choosing, to unlock us from conflict with each other. The principle of Providence leaves us free to apologize honestly and sincerely when we tire of inner conflict.

ASASE YE DURU

"The Earth has weight"

Nature sustains life.

Providence

We Live in a Benevolent Universe.

—Dr. Virginia A. Price

DEFY DIFFICULTIES
Persevere with resolve and grit.

One of the most difficult things to learn is how to defy difficulties. To stick our chins out and ball up our fists and say, "Bring it on!" We all enjoy challenges, of course. But really, we're after the payoffs that result from running the gauntlet successfully. What we really want are the spoils, the perks, the "bennies," and the "goodies."

To defy difficulties is to brave the hard stuff without hope of gaining any reward besides having survived an ordeal. What about the times when survival brings little joy? Estella Majozo noted just this situation in her epic poem, *The Middle Passage: 105 Days*, describing the awesome voyage of captured Africans brought to the Americas.

At those times, the choice to live, to survive, and to rise again requires defiance against difficulties. The African American culture would be different if our ancestors had been without this principle.

Suggested Activity
Learn more about the trials and tribulations of our African American ancestors who survived the Middle Passage.

Sometimes we forget that the most difficult challenges require reliance on spiritual forces. I was reminded of this when I was in Senegal to learn about how the Senegalese treated mental illness. I talked with the Western-trained Chief Psychiatrists at Dakar's university clinic and at the National Psychiatric Hospital. They told me that they were able to work much more effectively with Traditional Healers from the affected patient's village. The Traditional Healers, in turn, referred their most difficult cases to the N'Deup priestesses.

At Yoff, ancestral home of the Lebou people, I met with Arame Leye, the regional Chief Priestess of N'Deup to explore how the N'Deup priestesses used healing rituals to make people well. The Traditional Healers use plant medicine, which suffices for most illnesses. The priestesses, however, were trained from childhood to use spiritual means to manage problems that defied treatment. The Lebou believe that local ancestral spirits protect them from serious harm, and look to the priestesses to perform rituals that call on spirits to restore order to the community, especially damaged social relationships.

"Fern"

Hardy fern grows in difficult conditions.

Endurance & Resourcefulness

Mental toughness supports an indomitable spirit.

ABUNDANCE
Be open to others and willing to share your wealth.

Cola nuts are a cash crop from trees of the cocoa family. A cash crop is one that is easily salable for its properties. The cola nut is rich in caffeine. It has many health benefits, and is an ingredient in cough medicines. It also is used in soft drinks. Additionally, because of the traditional religious emphasis on health, bearing and raising children and wealth, cola nuts are used in naming ceremonies, weddings, funerals and divination rituals by numerous tribes. No wonder it is a symbol of affluence and abundance in Ghana, Nigeria and other tropical African countries.

Affluence has more to do with our openness to others than with wealth itself. I'm not a particularly superstitious person, but let me tell you about one of my favorite experiences of the principle of Affluence. I was sitting on the grass in a park watching my little ones playing. Another parent brought her children to play, and she sat near me and we began our conversation. She was one of the warmest, friendliest people I had ever met. She told me her name was Lucky. Her face was scarred from multiple surgeries following a terrible automobile accident that she barely survived. Yet, she was strangely unconcerned with her appearance. She began picking through the blades of grass. As we talked, she handed me a four-leaf clover. "Here." "Oh my goodness, that's great! You better keep it!" She laughed. "That's okay. I find them all the time," she said, picking up and showing me another. And another. People who practice affluence draw wealth to themselves—not so much for the sake of having it or saving it but for using and distributing it. Fortunately, this attitude, exemplified in the exhortations of such historical figures as the Buddha, Jesus the Christ, Francis of Assisi, and Mother Theresa, is acceptable as a healthy religious sentiment. "Share the wealth!"

Suggested Activity

Examine your attitudes toward wealth. How did they develop? What are your earliest memories about having enough food, warmth in winter, desserts and treats? Did you ever experience not having enough? Does money come easily to you? What do you do with it?

BESE SAKA

"Sack of cola nuts"

Plenty.

Affluence & Abundance

A good name is better than wealth.

PEACEMAKING
Strive for "win-win" and work for the good of all.

Getting along with others requires that we switch from an "I" perspective to a "we" perspective so that everyone's needs are met. Peacemaking is different from conflict resolution. Peacemaking is proactive. It's "going out of your way" to create conditions that benefit all concerned, which takes much thought and much work. "Blessed are the peacemakers."

Political scientists study how powerful people operate under different conditions. At the United Nations, they spend years watching how different wealthy nations' diplomats treat those from poorer countries. They follow the response of the key players to humanitarian crises among refugees in poor areas of the world. They keep up with how the key players vote to keep their own interests primary. They note that there is little that smaller, less influential countries can do to keep their interests in the discussion. They see that the more powerful nations determine the outcome of conflict even when everyone knows they are wrong. Peacemakers understand the pressure to allow the powerful to go unchallenged. They also understand that such a compromise is not wise because it is not just; it is not fair. The internal tension that injustice introduces into a situation becomes intolerable over time. When bullies and tyrants recognize this truth, peacemaking is possible.

> ### Suggested Activity
> **Familiarize yourself with some justice issues or areas in which arguments about fairness to one party are debated strongly in order to change the situation. Pick one as an area of study. Get involved with an organization that works for justice and peace around that issue. If you want peace, work for justice.**

Peacemakers must be able to tolerate ambiguity, to put up with being badly misunderstood. Peacemaking can be especially helpful during family conflict. Learn to make peace, to come up with solutions. Apologizing when you are wrong, asking for forgiveness, cleaning up your mess, and changing your actions is the way toward peace.

BI NKA BI

"No one should bite the other"

Image is two fish biting one another.

Peace & Harmony

Avoid provocation and strife.

STRATEGY
Make simple effective plans.

Y ou've got to have a plan. It doesn't make any difference whether you're trying to win a volleyball match, get into college, beat another player in a chess game, or take first place in a beauty pageant. You have to use strategy. A strategy is a plan designed to achieve an objective—what you want to achieve.

Businesses use strategy to position their products. Communities use strategy to prepare for emergencies to minimize loss of life and property. Generals use strategy to win wars. Battlefield strategy, for example, has many determinants, or pieces of the plan that affect the outcome—the terrain, or the type of field where the battle takes place; time of day to fight the battle; resources; climate and weather; weapons available; condition of the soldiers; and the soldiers' training and battle experience. Generals use their knowledge of these determinants and of the strengths and weaknesses of opposing troops to gauge chances of success.

> ## Suggested Activity
> **Make simple plans every day. Keep a schedule. Read a book on time management to learn to better manage your time.**

To get what you want, you need a plan of action. The simpler your plan, the better. When you develop your strategy, simplicity is key. When you plan the steps to include in your plan, be simple.

Think of yourself as an engineer. Engineers use scientific knowledge, math, and ingenuity to figure out solutions to technical, societal, and commercial problems. Imagine being an engineer whose job it is to figure out how to take home a volleyball trophy or get into college. Engineers know that the simpler the solution, the better. Sometimes, a single, simple solution may solve more than one problem, like, for example, by joining the debate club after school you learn to think and speak more clearly, which helps your grades and attracts friends because you are more interesting to listen to.

DAME-DAME

"A game of strategy"

A plan of action.

Intelligence & Ingenuity

Careful planning is the power of strategy.

ADAPTABILITY
Recognize when change is required.

Crocodiles have adapted to their environment for over 240 million years. They are nature's greatest survivors. We too must adapt to our environment. Instinct to run from dangers and to fight back is built in. To survive we must learn conditions that can harm us or help us survive. Parents teach us that the skull and cross-bones on a container means it is poisonous and can kill.

Our environment has many dangers, such as harm that can come from strangers. I remember walking into a classroom in a school where I was working to find two boys straightening out desks and erasing blackboards. As I entered, one boy looked at me, and alerted the other boy, "Stranger Danger." The boy was aware of the potential dangers from strangers and alerted his friend. Survival comes from seeing danger and preparing.

Suggested Activity

List the dangers you see in your environment around you? For each danger, imagine how you can survive it. Review your list frequently and mentally practice surviving each danger.

Guns and other weapons pose serious danger to survival. Many teens have access to firearms, but little training in using them. Just dropping a loaded pistol can lead to tragedy. Losing a brother or a sister to a gun shot is a terrible feeling. You can feel enraged and want to get even.

You also have an inner environment—thoughts and feelings. Thoughts, especially angry thoughts and sad thoughts can be dangerous for your survival. Like the boy who alerted his friend by saying, "Stranger Danger", you need to notice when you respond to events, like a snub from someone at school, with self-damaging thoughts, like "No one likes me"; or "I'll get him!" Angry thoughts, make you feel even more angry and encourage you to act in angry ways that put you in jeopardy. Self-defeating thoughts like, "I want to stop using drugs, but it's just too hard" undermine confidence and make you feel weak. Emotional thoughts can make you question your power to act purposefully; pushing you to act without thinking.

DENKYEM

"Crocodile"

The crocodile lives in water, but breaths air.

Adaptability

Survival skills can save your life.

CARING
Show caring through your acitons.

As a teen, I watched my mother and grandmother grow flowers. They loved African violets, roses, gladiolas and geraniums. They created places throughout the yard for colorful patches and rows of beautiful plants. They pruned and watered the plants and put food around the roots. They planted some flowers in the shade and others in the sun. They covered the plants in harsh weather. They helped me to understand that you have to care for plants to have beautiful flowers.

People are like plants. You show people you value them by how you care for them. You show caring by being gentle, thoughtful, generous, and nourishing. Being harsh, thoughtless, selfish, or mean is not caring. It's a contradiction to say you value a relationship that you systematically destroy, disregard, and withhold emotional support from them. That is a fundamental lie. It's like saying you love plants, but then withhold watering and let the sun burn its leaves.

You can't fool people about this. You can't fool yourself either. You can't say that you love and care for yourself if you do destructive, unthinking and poisonous things to yourself. People who say they love you, but treat you badly, slow your roll. Stop and think. Take your time. Talk to someone you trust about how these people make you feel. It takes time to learn to recognize people who fake caring to get what they want from you. Such people can be extremely convincing and can manipulate others without mercy, conscience, shame or regret. They may use tricks, such as playing stupid, whining, cajoling, lying, charming, crying and begging to break you down.

Take time getting to know who cares for you. Take your time getting to know whom you care for. It takes time and much learning to get caring figured out.

> ## Suggested Activity
> Make a list of people important to you. One by one imagine being with each person and notice how you feel. When you don't feel warm and caring, cross that person off the list. Repeat this exercise in a month to see if your list has gotten longer.

DUAFE

"Wooden comb"

There is beauty in combed hair.

Love and Caring

Show love through care.

STRENGTH & HUMILITY

Be gentle but firm.

Young people are often indulged. Parents may tell their children they are the strongest, the fastest, the quickest, the best. We let them win races. We slip and fall at the start. We let them catch up. For a while, we let them enjoy feeling like they will always win. But, soon enough, as their circle of friends grows, someone bursts the bubble of their invincibility. Someone beats them. It's a nasty surprise if you're not prepared.

Sports and other competitions teach how to handle losing. By participating in athletic competitions and joining sports teams, or science fairs, or spelling bees, you learn to lose with grace. Expecting to win all the time is unrealistic and sets you up for a crash.

> ## Suggested Activity
>
> **Practice hard, play hard.
> Always speak humbly of your
> accomplishments.**

A psychologist friend who works at a big corporation spends all day seeing brilliant young scientists who have had little experience with failing. From an early age, the young scientists were tutored and fawned over. They grew up like special flowers in a greenhouse. They graduated from college in their mid-teens and went into advanced programs. Everything went well for them until entering the corporate work world where the gifted scientists had to team play with others who were not so special. The scientists encountered personality conflicts, petty jealousies, and scrambles for power. They had never been ridiculed in the schoolyard. Young Black scientists were devastated by racist name-calling and distraught with depression and rage. My psychologist friend helped them to manage challenges to their self-esteem and sense of superiority.

Without experience in defeat, you don't know how to lose so you look like a poor sport. Showing grace means not falling apart because you didn't make the soccer team. It means not giving up because you didn't win a game against a cross-town rival. If you keep playing, competing, or being your best, you will experience defeats—along with many successes. Win with humililty; lose with grace.

DWENNIMMEN

"Ram's horns"

The ram's horns are graceful, yet it fights fiercely.

Humility Together with Strength

Unpretentious strength promotes success.

SET LIMITS
Look before you leap; think before acting.

A ten-year-old boy was visiting his classmate. On the way to pick up his son, the father encountered the boys three blocks from the friend's house. They were riding bikes in the middle of the street down a steep hill with large trees on each side, while giggling wildly, barely in control of their bikes. Concerned about their recklessness, the father made them walk the bikes back to the house, and reported what happened to friend's parents. Both boys received a strict punishment—no bikes for one week.

This episode could have ended in disaster. It was a busy street and they were not wearing helmets—or paying attention! We learn safety by watching what happens to others and, through experience, learning what happens to oneself. We learn safety "vicariously" by observing what happens when others drink and drive, for example; or play with electricity, swim in fast-moving water, and so on. By comparison we learn "through experience" when we encounter [not just watch] the actual consequences of our actions.

> ## Suggested Activity
> Write down the rules for home and street safety your parents taught you. How does the security of your parent's rules increase your feelings of love?

Acting with security and love means doing what you know is right—and being assured that those you love will understand. For example, a 13-year-old black girl was threatened with expulsion from school because she refused to be paddled by the teacher for a transgression. "Lean over the desk!" the teacher demanded. The girl politely refused. "But I'm not allowed to let you whip me," she responded.

The teacher became furious, her face turning red with anger and frustration as she repeated her demand, telling the girl she would be expelled if she refused. "I'd like to let you whip me just to get it over with, but you would really get into trouble," the girl continued.

The teacher relented, luckily, learning her lesson the easy way. The girl had been raised without physical punishment, and she had been taught that a lady does not permit anyone to raise a hand toward her. She knew it was unnecessary for her to submit to a paddling.

EBAN

"Fence"

A fence secures the family from the outside.

Boundaries

The ideal home has a fence around it.

JUSTICE
Do the right thing.

You take the test for a driver's license and pass. You listen to your parent's warnings and tell them to trust you. Then they give you the keys to the car! Now, you feel like you are on top of the world. And for a while you are!

Then, one day, it happens. You make one little slip-up. You go by a friend's house and drink a couple of beers while you play a video game. Then the two of you drive by another friend's house. This friend sees you coming, and jumps into the car with a couple of joints in his pocket. Life is good. The radio is on the right station. You're laughing and talking. You drive past a red light. A siren goes off. It's from that police car coming up behind you.

"Driver's license and registration, please." By the time he finishes with you, your car will be impounded, you and your friends will be in lock-up for reckless driving and endangerment, possession of illegal substances, and driving under the influence. Oh, and seatbelt infractions, too. The wheels of justice are about to run over you. Your family's costs for letting you drive the car suddenly rise. Will someone in your family have several hundred dollars on hand just for this occasion? You knew the rules, and you broke them. There will still be pain, because justice is a rough teacher: court costs, impoundment fees, lawyer fees, community service hours, higher insurance premiums and defensive driving courses, counseling, and last but not least, spending regular, undesired time with your probation officer.

Check local laws for what privileges you have. Laws are rules society makes so people behave in an orderly way. These rules would not be made unless they are necessary—and then only if they are to be enforced. If you ever have to break rules, you should have a good reason. Convenience is not a good reason.

Suggested Activity

Learn laws applicable for your age. Does your family expect you to follow these rules? What can happen if you disregard them, such as driving drunk, truancy, destruction of property, theft, or ignoring parental instructions for dating and curfews?

"Handcuffs"

Chiefs cuff offenders of the law.

Law & Justice

The law is uncompromising.

SUPPORT
Good friends help you become the best you.

When we make friends with someone, we create a bond, a connection with that person. The bond of friendships includes mutual affection and a desire to please the other person. This can be seen in our willingness to help our friend whenever we can. This is a strong impulse. Friendship, however, also entails the responsibility and willingness to set limits when necessary.

It is not proper to help a friend do wrong. This is called "enabling", which is especially damaging when people are enmeshed, or unlikely to act with a sense of their own integrity in a relationship. Enabling means that your actions make it possible for the other person to make unhealthy choices. For instance, if your friend frequently asks you to give her money to buy drugs, and you cannot resist her requests, you are enabling her. Being afraid to tell your friend that she is going down the wrong path is not okay either, because one day, you will feel that you could have done more for your friendship. We are able to act as our own person in a lot of ways, but it is possible to allow a friendship to become enmeshed, thus producing codependency. In codependent relationships, one person helps the other's addiction, delusional thinking, bad habits, under-achievement and irresponsibility.

Relying on your friends is one thing. Everyone wants to be able to lean on good friends. Creating codependency is another. True friends will not help you do wrong. An enabler will help you do wrong.

Sometimes we overload parents with the expectation that they should be their teens' best friends as well. Parents' relationship with their teen is based on their authority. A friend's relationship is more reliant on mutuality, sharing, and equality. Parents who bail out of the responsibility of authority can find themselves in court for neglect, endangerment, and contributing to the delinquency of a minor.

Suggested Activity

List your closest friends. Circle the ones with whom you have the most sharing and the most similar goals. Determine the reasons you keep friends who do not share your interests and goals.

ESE NE TEKREMA

"The teeth and the tongue"

The teeth and tongue work together.

Friendship & Interdependence

Use bonds of friendship to succeed.

INDEPENDENCE
By your decisions you transition to adulthood.

When you were a baby, you needed parents. You couldn't do anything without their help. Babies are nearly completely dependent on their parents. By the time you were two, you established a little independence, if only to say "No!" Psychologists refer to this time as "the terrible twos."

Gradually, you established yourself as someone who could be trusted to make good decisions. You could decide what to wear, when to go to the toilet.

By early childhood, you were able to make smart choices if the decisions were simple. Your entrance into higher learning environments at various ages marked your transitions from pre-school, grade school, middle school, and finally high school. At each level, you were expected to be more independent, and to need fewer directions. Your ability to make responsible decisions grows as you gain more trust from your parents and gain more independence. You learn to account for your choices in acceptable ways.

Your teen years are filled with opportunities to practice becoming more independent. You can learn to travel about by bus or by subway, you can go to a movie by yourself, or ride a bicycle to the neighborhood park—by yourself. These activities are some of the ways you demonstrate that you can handle yourself responsibly. By the time you are 18, you legally are able to make big decisions independently. You are allowed to decide, more or less independently, how you want to do to make a living, whom you want to marry, where you want to live, and when you want to come and go.

The road from dependence to independence is full of twists and turns. Road signs become complex and costs for a wrong turn keep rising. Risks are greater. Navigating the transition with grace, accepting responsibility for the outcome of our choices is what shows that we are becoming adults.

> ## Suggested Activity
> Write down the steps you use when making a big decision. How do you set your goals? Gather information? Assess and compare your alternatives?

FAWOHODIE

"Independence"
Emancipation.

Independence & Freedom

Independence is rooted in responsibility.

CIRCUMSPECTION
Use good judgement to avoid danger.

One of or most basic needs is to feel safe and secure. There are many ways to achieve this feeling. For example, we can stay only around people whom we know will love and protect us. We can "buy" their love, with extravagant gifts to keep them close. Some people hire bodyguards or join gangs to feel safe and secure. Others keep large amounts of cash available at all times. Still others won't let go of one boyfriend until they have another one securely in hand. Whatever the form our method of finding safety and security takes, fulfilling the need for safety and security can be an elusive goal. When the need is severe, it can express itself as an emotional disorder. We may need therapeutic help. For example, post-traumatic stress from sexual abuse, rape, strong-arm robbery, house invasion, severe beating—any of these experiences can unleash the feeling that we are not safe.

When our feelings of safety and security have been compromised, or when we feel we have been violated, we respond with fear and anger, and sometimes panic. We become more protective about whom we let into our space.

> ### Suggested Activity
>
> **Assess your resources for getting some good advice? Whom do you call at times of stress and confusion and hurt? We all need someone we trust to help us learn to heal and to begin to learn how to feel safe again. Find that person you will call.**

We become more discerning, more discriminatory about whom we open up to. We begin to police our heart as carefully as an Akan compound house that has only one main way in and out, letting in only those who seem safe. It may take a long time before we feel safe enough to let anyone else in again.

Working past the pain may require talking to a trusted counselor trained to help people treat such problems. Many people, for example, have lasting memories of trauma from sexual abuse and rape. The memories can cripple them if they let them fester inside. The important thing is to begin the process of healing by talking about ways to overcome them and sharing the associated thoughts and feelings.

FIHANKRA

"House/Compound"

The housing compound has only one entrance.

Security & Safety

Prudence and caution keep risk in check.

SHARING
Understand giving to others as symbiosis and reciprocity.
—Estella Conwill Majozo

As children, we learn the importance of sharing. We share food; our parents' time; our teachers' attention; toys; pews in church; the earth.

Sharing is when you have a candy bar and I don't, so you split your candy bar with me. Reciprocity is when I do the same for you when I have a candy bar and you don't. Reciprocity is when you are down and out, and know that I will lend you a hand to help you get back on your feet. Reciprocity is when you know you can ask me to help you build your kitchen cabinets because I gave up all my evenings for a week to help you with your floors.

> ## Suggested Activity
>
> The next time a homeless person asks you for spare change, reflect on how you feel about it. What are your rules for sharing money? Do you give to the "impaired" but not to the able bodied? Do you give only to mothers who are poor, without the support of men? Do you give only to nonprofits?

Symbiosis is an altogether different concept from sharing and reciprocity. Symbiosis is creative and exciting. With symbiosis, both you and your friend can achieve much more together than either of you could accomplish separately. Symbiosis is when you both bring your complementary talents and skills together, and greatly expand the possibilities resulting from working together. The symbiotic relationship between candle-maker William Procter and soap-maker James Gamble began when they put their resources together in 1837. Later, they got a contract to supply the Union Army with candles and soap during the Civil War. They marketed a floating soap called "Ivory" during the 1880s, sponsored "soap operas" on radio during the 1920s, and were associated with many other popular products. In 2014, Procter & Gamble recorded $83 billion in sales. Another outstanding example of symbiosis is Apple Computer founders Steve Wozniak and Steve Jobs. There are also great examples of symbiosis in the music industry. Look for opportunities for symbiosis in your life.

FUNTUNFUNEFUDENKYEMFUNEFU

"Siamese crocodiles"

Siamese crocodiles share one stomach, yet fight over food.

Democracy & Unity

Tribal infighting is harmful.

SERVE OTHERS
Give what you can—take what you need. —Kinshasha Holman Conwill

Volunteers are special people who do what has to be done to make things work even when they don't receive money for helping. They work at schools, hospitals, churches, and all sorts of other organizations. They give tours at museums, care for animals at zoos, train dogs to visit people in institutions, cook food for the hungry on holidays, coach children's sports, and organize fundraising for nonprofit organizations.

Not long ago, I began working with an organization of mostly very poor mothers concerned with the most basic needs of their children in their community. The mothers formed the organization in response to the staggering lack of resources to insure the safety of their children, especially as they walked back and forth to school. Members of the organization decided to place observers along the sidewalks throughout the neighborhood to assure the children of proper supervision. They posted signs declaring the area a safety zone before and after school. Suddenly, the dangers of sidewalk violence disappeared.

Suggested Activity

Select your favorite nonprofit agency. Volunteer four hours a week in the agency for a few months. What happened at the agency because of your involvement?

When School Board officials visited the school site and discovered the safety monitors, they asked, "Who is paying them?" On learning that the monitors were volunteers, the officials requested that the School Board be allowed to pay them! Whenever we see good-hearted service, we all want to jump in and help!

One of my favorite volunteers, a tough, fair, gutsy lady who played championship-quality basketball in college, explained why she works so hard without being paid money. She said, "It's our turn to take care of things."

Voluntarism is not mainly about not getting paid. Voluntarism means stepping forward to take care of a problem because it needs to be addressed. Without voluntarism, too much would be left undone.

NEA OPE SE OBEDI HENE

"He who wants to be king "

Serving the community.

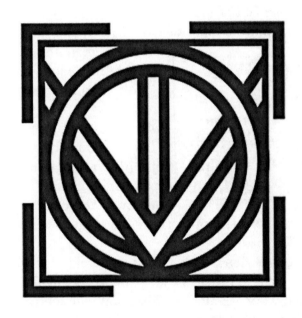

Service & Leadership

To be king, learn to serve.

FAITH

Be immovable; expect the mountain to move.

Most of us think about an organized religion like Islam, Christianity, Judaism, or Buddhism when we think of faith. But more generally, faith means being able to rely on a higher power in our daily lives—and being able to broaden our natural resources to otherwise unimaginable dimensions.

Our ancestors, many of them unnamed and forgotten, survived inhumane capture and enslavement only because of their ability to rely on their faith. Their steadfast faith enabled them to give us the legacy of life.

Sometimes we hear the phrase "leap of faith". We make that leap when we've exhausted our human efforts at understanding, and we accept the divine helping hand.

> ## Suggested Activity
>
> **Reflect on your family's faith as your heritage. Thank your parents for teaching you their faith, and a relationship to the Divine and to each other through faith.**

Faith can be measured by the quality and the intensity of our prayer. Mumbling prayers with arms outstretched may look good at church and in the movies, but true prayers full of faith are much different. True faith means full abandonment to our Higher Power, or to our God. The closer we get to this level of faith, the more fervent and powerful our prayer becomes, the less selfish our motivation, and the stronger our belief.

Faith can be seen in your actions. Sometimes, you hear "Let go and let God handle it." When you have faith, you behave in ways that show it. Remaining calm, working steadily towards an outcome even when it's unlikely that you will achieve it in your lifetime, and trusting that good will come out of your efforts—these too are signs of faith, sometimes referred to as belief in things unseen.

Faith is a kind of trust you maintain even when your rational mind does not agree. One of our nation's greatest citizens, The Rev. Dr. Martin Luther King, was a man of faith. "Faith can move mountains."

NSOROMMA

"Child of the heavens [stars]"

God is the father and watches over all people.

Guardianship & Faith

Use powerful fervent prayer.

GOD IS HERE
Rise to peak performance through contemplation.

Our levels of awareness—or states of consciousness—can change from one moment to the next. Maintaining an optimal level of constancy of awareness of God's presence is the work of contemplation and meditation. It is difficult to stay at a high level of awareness with all the distractions of daily life, and so it is important to schedule times of quiet and peace regularly. Eventually, the most dedicated of us reach a point where we can become contemplatives. We are able to spend longer periods of time in awareness of the presence and protection of God throughout our daily activities.

Becoming a contemplative is somewhat like becoming a basketball superstar. Only a few of the best professional basketball players become superstars. They are the ones who can play hard a whole game without losing concentration and intensity. They are aware of the clock, the score, the play and its options, the movement on the floor, the number of team fouls, the defensive shifts that their opponents used on prior times down court, and a host of other factors that influence the outcome of each play. The superstars are able to ignore thoughts about a sick child at home or a spouse delivering a baby. They can tune out rude gestures by fans, shaking pom-poms, jeers, trash talk, and jitters for forty-eight minutes.

> ## Suggested Activity
>
> **There are many ways to meditate. Learn one. Learn and practice being relaxed and aware at the same time. Spend time regularly in the presence of God.**

Just as it takes the superstar many years of dedicated practice to learn to play "in the zone" for a whole game, it takes time for the contemplative to learn how to relax in the presence of God.

Meditation is the practice of relaxing in the presence of God or focusing on the awareness that we are part of something bigger than we are. Meditation is "being in the zone." Meditation practice eventually enables us to relax under pressure, to feel calm in the midst of chaos, and to remain attentive to our main objectives with less distraction.

NYAME DUA

"Tree of god — altar"
Where we perform rituals.

God's Presence & Protection
Know who you are.

HOPE
Drop an anchor to allow storms to pass you by.

An anchor is a symbol for hope. Ancient mariners understood that sometimes all they could do in a storm was haul in the sails, throw the anchor overboard, and hang on for dear life until the storm passed. The anchor kept the boat in place, protecting it from being slammed into rocky crags.

Sailors trusted that if the ship sustained major damage when the storm passed they could make it to a safe harbor for repair. An attitude of hope is a virtue we should cultivate because it enables us to set goals with confidence that we will not be thrown off course irretrievably.

Hope is a value we find in Gospel songs and other Black Church music. Reliance on divine assistance is a sentiment expressed in the Brazilian proverb: "Don't tell God that you have a great problem. Tell your problem that you have a great God." In a chapter in the book, *Butterfly Blessings in the Face of Cancer*, I described medical studies on interactions among positive thoughts regarding disease outcomes and the body's defenses that have led to an emphasis on increasing patients' sense of hope while undergoing treatment. Patients with hope fare better and live longer.

> ### Suggested Activity
> Find out how anchors work and read some of the rules followed on ships at sea.

With hope, we can set long-term goals even if we may not live to see their realization. Without hope, people are not likely to undertake tasks they might finish in the distant future. Examples of people living with hope are all around, including people who plan projects that take years to complete; people who decide to have babies; people who go on long trips to learn a new language; and people who plan to get married. Looking forward to good outcomes, they all make their plans, gather their resources, ready themselves, keeping their eyes on guideposts along the journey.

Sustaining ourselves by maintaining hope is an important aspect of living. We keep hope alive by nourishing a healthy spiritual life with prayer and meditation, by helping and encouraging others, and by being grateful for what is good in our lives rather than bemoaning what we feel is missing.

NYAME BIRIBI WO SORO

"God is in the heavens"

God listens to all prayers.

Trust and Faith

Expect the best.

INFINITY OF THE SOUL
Cultivate positive emotions.

The infinity of the soul is usually understood in the sense that the soul—the part of us that informs our physical existence as a person—continues on after our physical death. The infinity of the soul also can be understood as extending along other dimensions—and not just the temporal. Let's think of the principle of the infinity of the soul as it speaks about time, with death as the limit; let's also understand the infinity of the soul as the it extends beyond a person's skin as its boundary. In other words, we can also understand the soul's infinity to mean that the soul extends beyond the measured spatial confines of the living body. This is a common theme in literature and science.

> ## Suggested Activity
> Take a meditation class and practice diligently for a few years before you become an adult.

For example, beloved and devoted friends somehow "enter" each other's souls, transcending, or going beyond, their sense of individuality and "apartness" from each other that we normally feel. And at those moments, they feel ecstatic, like they are outside the limits of their bodies. They feel buoyant and expansive; as if their souls have burst loose from the spatial confines of their bodies.

This type of "boundlessness" of the soul is usually most apparent when we experience positive emotions—triumph, contentment, joy, and happiness. I'm reminded of this sometimes when I see extremely happy people barely containing themselves, jumping around as if they can fly. Highly positive emotional experiences feel wonderful, and we try to hold onto these moments when we feel outside ourselves. Contemplation and meditation are important because these practices can teach us to maintain these positive emotional states, thereby enhancing our awareness of the infinity of the soul.

Extremely negative emotions, on the other hand, bring sensations of dense heaviness. Teens can learn to manage their emotions by experimenting with thoughts that bring on buoyant, positive feelings. Keeping track of what you feel, and paying attention to what you think when you experience positive or negative emotions is a way you can learn to maintain happy, buoyant feelings.

NYAME NNWU NA MAWU

"God never dies, therefore I cannot die"

Man's soul is immortial.

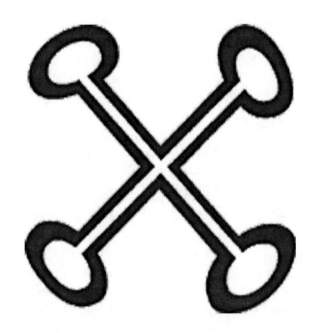

God is omnipresence

The soul rests with God.

TRUST IN GOD
Base your relationships on loving behavior.

The appeal of great love stories is a promise that our love for another is not bounded by age, culture, or class—that love is bigger than death! This promise makes stories of loving relationships special. It is in relationships that we most easily recognize God:—love between a parent and a child, a wife and a husband, or two best friends. Loving behavior engenders healthy relationships, and healthy relationships engender trust. Trust enables us to relax deeply when relationships are based on loving behavior because we know everything will work out well.

Religion usually provides a kind of "firm ground" for those who believe that all things work for the good. However, when we think about Trust in God outside the context of a particular faith tradition, with its foundation of sacred texts like the Bible, we may find ourselves in unfamiliar territory. In these cases, we can substitute "Trust in God" for trust in a victorious force for good in the universe.

Suggested Activity

Attend classes on your religion. How do they portray God? As an angry, vengeful destroyer? As a forgiving judge? As a loving parent? This is important because it gives you a key to understanding your training to react to bad things happening in your life.

Some events can shake our trust in God. The sudden death of a child, or the murder of a friend can leave us wondering what kind of God allows such a terrible events. We can become angry with God.

To regain lost trust, we must acknowledge the pain of loss at least enough to talk about it and share the pain with someone we trust. Then, we must reach outside ourselves, connecting with others who might need our help, and re-creating community with those around us instead of isolating ourselves. We actively must break out of our sense that this has happened only to us. Finally, we must focus on the good things, the positive things in our lives. It may take months for the pain to subside. If we don't know this, we may be tempted to act rashly and destructively instead of waiting patiently for relief from our anger and pain.

NYAME NTI

"By God's grace"
God has provided us this stalk to eat.

Faith & Trust in God

The stalk is the staff of life.

PRAISE GOD
God's presence is constant.

According to the principle of "God is King", we're here to bring good into the world—not evil and divisiveness. With this as a prime objective, we will not stray far off course before correcting ourselves. We will shun inclinations to engage in destructive behaviors that harm others and ourselves.

Many people would agree that our biggest priority is protecting our children from harm. It's something we could all stand behind. However, as the saying goes, "The devil is in the details" means it's easy to agree in general about issues, but when it comes to hammering out specifics, there are lots of sticking points. It's the same for ethics.

We have to constantly stay alert to changes in the demands of the situation, struggling with what emerges as a priority. It's not easy. Some instances of taking account of priorities can be seen in Family Court decisions, for example, where "the good of the child" is listed as the guiding principle in decision-making, and the judge allows a child to choose the custodial parent. Others instances can be found at those times when mothers risk losing their lives to

---

Suggested Activity

Each day strive to get rid of behavior that makes fun of or puts down others. Let this principle guide you every day.

---

bring a child into the world. We hear of people who break laws and promises when they decide that one guiding principle should take precedence over another.

Deliberately causing harm, destroying the character and good work of others, plotting evil deeds, and forcing your will onto others are contrary to the principle of "God Is King." Every so many years across the ages, we develop new mythologies to take the place of the old ones, to expound this principle of living judiciously as good people. They remind the young to choose good order over destruction, chaos and death. From the Archangel Michael and his angelic hosts against Lucifer and his demonic minions, cast down for their pride, to Optimus Prime and his Transformers against Megatron and his Decepticons, the stories warn each generation to end destruction and to bring about peace.

NYAME YE OHENE

"God is King "

Greatness and power.

Majesty & Supremacy of God

God is supreme authority.

INTELLIGENCE
Practice mindfulness.

Intelligence is shown, generally, by the way we solve problems that confront us in everyday life. Problems are solved most easily when we are in a mindful state. You enter this state by stepping back to see the setting of the problem, viewing it from a variety of perspectives, responding in a "natural" or unforced way, and by recognizing when the correct solution presents itself. The mindful state makes it easier to associate the conditions that represent the problem with the solution that corresponds to our intended outcome.

We measure some forms of intelligence by performing certain tasks on tests. We demonstrate others by creating works of art. Still others are demonstrated in how we perform in social relationships, athletic competitions, or parlor games. The idea is to respond to conditions that challenge us in functional ways.

Suggested Activity

List the challenges have you met successfully up through this point in your life? What problem-solving methods do you prefer? Read a book on problem solving.

Sometimes, problem-solving requires enough information and training to act effectively in a situation. People operating at this level get the information based on their need-to-know. Judges, for example, assign psychologists to write court reports so they can decide what to do with teens whose behavior is confusing to them. These court-related psychologists ask embarrassing questions, and expect truthful answers. They ask these questions based on their need-to-know.

At other times, problem-solving is simply a matter of doing the right thing, or resisting the pressure to look the other way or do someone a favor. Anytime we are asked to bend the rules and regulations for someone, you can bet that we are being asked to allow something unfair to happen. Giving in to that pressure sets a precedent that we will have to answer for. That's called being irresponsible, and sets us up for criticism unless we have the authority to break the rules. Usually, rule-breaking authority resides at the top.

That's why we want smart people at the top of organizations. Smart people are those who are able to recognize when and why a rule should be broken in a particular situation.

NYANSAPO

"Trust your inner wisdom "
A wise person chooses the best means to attain a goal.

Wisdom & Intelligence

Experience, knowledge and good judgement.

TENDERNESS
Be gentle.

Whatever we do—and whatever is done to us—that makes a mess of things will not be worth holding on to for very long. Period. Treating others with tenderness is a way to remember this.

Sometimes treating ourselves tenderly is harder than treating others with tenderness because of our attachment to our self-image of perfection. Self-pity is a way of wallowing in mud because we've found a little spot on our clothes. Treating ourselves with tenderness means getting the spot cleaned and going on about our way.

Tenderness is a mark of greatness of soul. We all need so much healing today that we should strive to practice tenderness as a discipline. Justifying cruelty and disrespect because of what someone has done is counterproductive. Tenderness heals. We use tenderness to care for wild animals, wounded birds, abused dogs, and horses in need of training, yet balk when it comes to ourselves, our children at home, at school, and in the streets. We see examples, terrible examples of cruel treatment every day. Brutally kicking and attacking a child for having a bad day at school or for wetting her pants, beating up a homeless person whose very presence reminds us that life can be unfair through no fault, making fun of someone who is physically challenged, intellectually, or emotionally —these cruel impulses show we are a long way from realizing that we all are vulnerable. Our cruelty to others counters our own fears of vulnerability. Until we address those fears, we will see little wrong with the harm we cause through our hard-hearted indifference to the suffering of others.

The 12th century founder of the Franciscans, Francis of Assisi, was noted for his love of animals and the environment, as well as his love for the poor, dedicated his life to helping us understand that we should see that we are all brothers and sisters.

Suggested Activity

Keep a diary for a couple months. Look back on it a few months from now. How many things don't seem important anymore?

ODO NNYEW AE KWAN

"Love never loses its way home"

Make room for tenderness in your spirit.

Tenderness

Let compassion be your guide.

POWER
You have the potential to change things.

There are many forms of power. Political power, for instance, enables the many to impose their will onto the few. Moral power sometimes enables the weak to resist the force of the strong by invoking the awareness of wrongdoing in the latter. Intellectual power allows the forward thinking to fashion new and better ways of solving old problems. We apply power to move things, to motivate ourselves, to achieve our goals.

Your basic power is the ability to define yourself: who you are, what you do, how you do it, when you do it, and where you do it. When you feel you can do something, you make your move. If someone tricks you into feeling you can do nothing, you do nothing.

Suggested Activity

Break your most salient bad habit, starting now. Study our music, our art, and our philosophy.

I recall talking with a tall, athletic, handsome 14-year-old who was in serious trouble for hitting a classmate who called him gay. He got so angry that he hit him in the jaw. "Well, are you gay?" I asked. He was shocked by my quesiton. "No!" he stated emphatically. "Well, if you were gay, would you still have hit him?" The question stumped him. I explained that his classmate didn't care if he was gay, rather he knew that he could make him mad by calling him gay. The light in his mind clicked on so that he was thinking about the experience of being upset instead of just reacting to the affront.

"Your classmate is probably jealous. Others cheer for you on the basketball court, you have a team jacket, and girls talk about you. He tricked you into hitting him by calling you gay. You fell for it," I explained. He got it.

Don't give up your power to someone jerking you around. When you are afraid of being called gay, or a scared-y cat, or a virgin, getting jerked around can get you pregnant, thrown off the team, suspended from school, arrested, convicted, and jailed. Where's your hook that people can grab to jerk you around? Don't give up your power.

OKODEE MMOWERE

"The talons of the eagle"

The eagle is the mightiest bird in the sky.

Strength, Bravery, Power

Balance strength with beauty.

FAITHFULNESS
Be dependable and trustworthy.

Faithfulness is not just being consistent about what you say you believe in. Faithfulness calls for commitment and disciplined practice of the principles of your beliefs. This means getting up in the morning with an awareness of what is important to you as a person, a family member, a friend, and a citizen—and living accordingly on a moment-to-moment basis. There is something magical in a person who has learned how to live like this. Such a person has learned to apply each and every ounce of energy into committing herself to an ethical life.

Living like this tends to cut down on the number of times you must apologize for acting mindlessly or feel ashamed for not measuring up to the reasonable expectations of your family, church, school, or society.

> **Suggested Activity**
>
> Relate your daily activities to the principles taught in your family. What values are you expressing faithfully?

We all make mistakes. We all have acted in ways to hurt others. Sometimes we are aware of this. At other times, we allow our defense mechanisms such as denial and blaming others to protect ourselves against awareness. When you realize the hurtfulness of your actions and the pain you have caused, you must pause and correct yourself, whether through apology or repair of the damage.

Sometimes the hurt is directed purposely against someone close, such as a spouse, or a brother and sister. Sometimes, it's leveled against a friend. Sometimes against those you don't even know. Leaving the hurt to fester is very destructive. Ugly words meant to cripple the spirit of others, insults designed to make others feel small or worthless, and refusals to apologize even when you know you wronged others are not signs of strength. Instead, they indicate a brittleness of spirit that hides a hardened refusal to look inward to your faults. It is our pride in causing pain and hurting others that is the shame

OSRAM NE NSOROMMA

"The Moon and the Star"

The North Star waits for return of the moon, her husband.

Love, Faithfulness, Harmony

A man and a woman.

PERSISTENCE
Train hard every day.

Several years ago, I met a young man at a conference who told me he was dyslexic. He was interested in advanced study so he could learn to help young boys who had dyslexia. I advised him to work a year, prepare to take the entry tests, and apply to a program where he could find a mentor who could work with him through difficult times. As someone who had life-long problems with reading, he would need an ally to ward off faculty who wanted to dismiss him from a competitive advanced educational program. The next year I met him again at the conference. He had followed my advice. After six years of study, marriage and a baby, he had devised an approach for training children with dyslexia to read. Along the way, he gave himself a nickname: "Relentless".

With the help of faculty, mentors, and friends, he achieved his goal. He brought his relentless spirit to the game every single day. He was rewarded with a Ph.D., the highest educational degree in most fields, in recognition of his work.

I continued to follow "Relentless" for a while longer. He met every challenge with courage and an unrelenting spirit. He convinced even those who had discouraged his dreams of developing into a scholar that his research was onto something. He compared the results of his methods to those of other experts. He became a force with whom to reckon. He delivered lectures on his findings at every opportunity. He influenced educational directors, superintendents, and principals. He showed them that those children whom they had given up on were capable of learning how to read. He was invited to present his work at a national conference at the White House. He gave parents hope in their children with a diagnosis of dyslexia.

Suggested Activity

Think about what you want to accomplish and pick a nickname to represent your goal. Use your nickname to encourage and remind yourself of your goal. Tell your friends to call you by your nickname. Be relentless!

OWO FORO ADOBE

"Snake climbing the raffia tree"

Thorns on the tree are dangerous challenge for the snake.

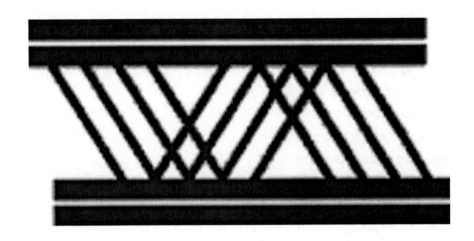

Steadfastness & Diligence

Persist with caution.

DEATH
Live each day as if it is the last one.

There are many ways to die. Dying suddenly without warning from heart attack. Dying immediately in a traffic accident or plane crash. Different religions, and thus different cultures, use many mechanisms to help us cope with fear of death. For example, various cultures have built pyramids, cathedrals, temples, mosques and monuments to inspire their descendants and to stand the test of time.

People join religious movements that connect them to those who have gone before and to those yet to be born. Doctors perfect plastic surgery techniques to deny aging. Scientists create death-defying technologies in the hopes of bringing people back to life. Finally, for those who can't afford the same amenities as the affluent, we change laws to allow assisted suicide so that even a poor person can manage the fear of death by taking control over when he dies.

Some of these mechanisms help us live worry-free and strive for good. Others may be more problematic. Some religions and cultures insist that everyone believe the same way, or risk condemnation, as the issue of whether assisted suicide is legal reveals.

Even in the US, a country founded on Freedom of Religion, old ways of protecting ourselves from the fear of death and uncertainty prevail. For example, controversial cultural beliefs about death evoke claims that the United States of America was founded as a Christian country—religious freedom was the goal. Who is "right" about what happens to us at the moment of death is not nearly as relevant as whether we can release ourselves from living without fear for the future and regret for the past. Each of us has to stay in that moment and let it pass.

Suggested Activity

Every few days think about what your faith says about death. Does it affect your ability to live fully in the present? If so, balance these distressing thoughts by focusing each day on the good all around you.

OWUO ATWEDEE

"The ladder of death"

Existence is transitory.

Mortality

Live a good life to prepare for afterlife.

READINESS
Be prepared.

Readiness is contextual: Ready for what? Readiness to do something is the active aspect of readiness. There is also a passive, or receptive aspect of readiness expressed in proverbs, like "When the student is ready, the teacher will appear," "The harder I work, the luckier I get" and one of my favorite, "Fortune favors the prepared mind."

Scientists are familiar with this passive notion of readiness as they double check observations. They specify the physical and environmental conditions such as temperature, lighting, instruments and machines used, and time of day. They put their observations into a context, and catalogue them. They make guesses as to what seems to be associated with it. They come up with hypotheses or intriguing propositions or statements about these guesses that may or not be true.

Suggested Activity

Prepare your mind every day. Be ready, front and center, every day. Show up. Pay attention.

Scientists design ways to test their hypotheses, and examine their results. They reject, or get rid of theories that do not improve your understanding of what is going on, and keep other theories to further test. When scientists come up with findings that point to the root cause of a phenomenon—whether it be teen pregnancy, gang violence, a weather system, police shootings, a virus, school absences, seasonal employment rates, civil uprisings, or childhood leukemia—they let other scientists see how they came up with their conclusions so they can review and test the results themselves. Sometimes all their scientific efforts get debunked or disproved.

The best scientists don't stay in the game to be right all the time. That's not how it works. That's not how any of this works. They stay in the game for the excitement of discovery. They play for that moment of serendipity—that fortunate stroke of luck when a scientist finds out the valuable key to understanding the phenomenon by chance, almost accidentally. It takes a prepared mind to recognize when that moment has arrived.

PEMPAMSIE

"Sew in readiness"
Show up every day.

Preparedness, Steadfastness

Be prespared.

PRACTICAL KNOWLEDGE
Conflict, confusion, and crisis are opportunities.

Experience is a hard taskmaster, from which not everyone learns easily. Some lessons are more difficult to learn than others. Sometimes the students are not as bright. Either way, experience is always teaching the lessons we need to master.

Teens sometimes figure they don't need to listen to the advice of their parents about lifestyle issues. "It's a new day," they say. "You've had your turn, you didn't do all that well. You're not rich. You don't have any friends. You don't like your job. You're divorced. You're not happy. You're old. Now it's our turn and we'll do it our way." The first teen I heard say this to his parent was hobbling about on crutches, with marks from several bullets on his torso. As an adult, he could be squeezed for information by threats of long jail terms after selling drugs for a few years. As his 18th birthday was approaching, he had been targeted for elimination. He had lost his car and his penthouse apartment while he was in the hospital. He couldn't wait to get back on the street, and get it all back. People couldn't tell whether he was a Wall Street lawyer or a drug dealer when he put a suit on, he explained, and his briefcase was just as pretty as theirs. For him, living large was more important than anything else. There was no arguing. He walked away.

> ## Suggested Activity
> Break your most salient bad habit, starting now. Study our music, our art, and our philosophy. What lessons do they hold for you?

The certitude of some people when they make such self-destructive decisions breaks down in the long run, and they return to tell the rest of us that they made a big mistake. Others are not so lucky they can come back.   There is an old saying: "Those who do not remember the past are doomed to repeat it." To keep from repeating past mistakes, you must be honest in recalling the events. The courage—and skill—to assess yourself objectively develops slowly. Be honest and accept responsibility for destructive behavior and damaged relationships, and diminish the contempt from others.

SANKOFA

"Reach back and get it"

It is not wrong to go back for that which you have forgotten.

Learn from the Past

Reflect on the past to build a successful future.

IMPROVE YOURSELF
Push your limits to become a bigger person.

There are many ways to transform yourself, to re-make yourself. Psychologists watch people change right before their eyes sometimes. It's always a pleasant surprise to realize over and over again how simple it all is. The behavioral change usually comes from suddenly seeing something that appears to be apparent to everybody else, and acting accordingly. For example, a mother demands that her previously suave husband leave their home immediately after suddenly becoming aware that her daughter's continuing reports about her husband's sexual advances toward her were true, or an angry self-pitying stroke victim wishing for her neglectful live-in son to wait on her realizes under questioning that the only person she was hurting by her refusal to work with her rehab team was herself.

> ## Suggested Activity
>
> **Question your beliefs about your character. Question your beliefs about your ability to change your bad habits. Above all, question your beliefs about how long things takes.**

As a martial arts practitioner, I have seen people make wonderful changes too. I was once working with a reserved, young White man with impressive fighting skills. One day, I took two of my sons, high school wrestlers, to a judo tournament he also attended. I introduced them. They all got along fabulously. The young man told them his story. His father had beaten him regularly when he was a child, thinking it would make him tough, and placed him in karate classes. "You're small. You aren't going to get much bigger. You've got to learn how to fight. Otherwise Black guys will really beat you up. They're mean." Then he added, "I was afraid of your father when I first met him. But now, I know my father was wrong. Your father is the nicest man in the world. I'm not afraid of Black guys anymore."

"Pushing your limits" can mean trying to do your personal best all the time. It can mean being patient instead of reacting with frustration when you are angry. That's the way to make break-throughs.

SESA WO SUBAN

"Change or transform your character "

Climb a tall tree to get a good view.

Life transformation

A star is a new start in the rotating wheel.

POSSESSIVENESS
Envy eats your spirit.

When we feel fear of losing someone or something important, simply expressing the emotion is rarely enough. Our loved one can work countless hours to save money and prepare for the future. If we're not getting enough time with our friend and respond with jealousy, it may seem selfish or unreasonable. Many folks believe jealousy is a bad emotion—the green-eyed monster—not a healthy emotion, which tends to make us feel ashamed when we argue about needing more time together. We're told the cause of jealousy is our lack of confidence, and not anything our loved one might be doing to merit our mistrust.

They may say, "Your girlfriend wants to go to college and you're all upset because she might find someone else and forget about you," or "You're childish and afraid worrying that she will grow apart if you don't go to school yourself," or "If your boyfriend takes that job, he will be around girls that are prettier and smarter than you are, and he will not want you anymore." Such feelings of inadequacy and insecurity can be frightening. We can envy what we imagine the rival has that sets us at

> ### Suggested Activity
> **Write a list of what you want in a meaningful relationship. Discuss your lists with someone you trust.**

a disadvantage. Girls may roll their eyes and tell their friends, "she thinks she is cute with all that long hair" and guys may hint that "even if he got that boss car, his game is still weak" to disparage the competition—feeling superior at that moment, then ashamed and small later.

Learning to manage jealousy takes time, and is especially difficult during teen years. We do not get a great deal of access to healthy teen models that handle jealousy well. Television and movies show jealous teens who have not learned to overcome the challenge of jealousy. They slash tires, key cars, cut into leather car seats, spread lies, and "beat down" their rivals. With healthy development, however, we recognize when we are acting out of a sense of shame, inadequacy or sick narcissism when we act out destructively. Loving ourselves fearlessly is a first step in learning to manage jealousy

TAMFO BEBRE

"The enemy will stew in his own juice"

Calm your emotions before they burn you up.

Jealousy & Envy

Covet not.

TOUGHNESS
You've got to have grit.

If you turn your TV to boxing, you see a lot of menacing, heavily muscled "tough guy" contestants strutting around, scowling and posturing. They get into each other's faces during weigh-ins, holding up their fists as if to promise to beat each other to a pulp. College and professional football and basketball teams are admonished to not unleash the other team's ire by challenging their toughness. "Leave it all on the field" is telling the team to focus their energy on the contest.

I once asked a military combat veteran what toughness meant. He related it immediately to someone who can "finish the job." He didn't mention anything about boys being more qualified for certain tasks than girls, strength training through CrossFit programs, heavier bodies generally outlasting lighter bodies by the end of a football game, being physically gifted, or being coachable. Just to "Who can get the job done?"

When I was a child, I read a lot about explorers and adventurers. I marveled at the exploits of people like Lewis and Clark's guide York, Jean Batiste Du Sable, and Matthew Hensen. As I got older, I added Harriet Tubman, Fanny Lou Hamer, Reginald K. Lewis, Mae Jemison and Ronald McNair to the mix. They all were tough. Toughness has nothing to do with gender, size, weight, skill level, or quality of preparation for a task. Toughness is a quality of the spirit. If you are a brittle, fearful person, your form breaks down—and you fall apart when you attempt a stressful task. If you are tough, you focus on completing tasks.

Toughness can be learned over time, usually through placing the learner into progressively demanding situations in which retreat and surrender are not allowed. Toughness is an important personal quality because it enhances reliability. In a group task, trust in the toughness of one's cohorts strengthens the probability of achieving an objective because it increases interdependency. No one wants to let the team down.

Suggested Activity

Join a team in a competitive league. There are softball, bowling, golf, track, and other teams out there for you to learn toughness. Play hard.

WAWA ABA

"Seed of the wawa tree"

The seed is extremely hard.

Hardiness & Endurance

Be strong and tough.

SUPPORTIVENESS
Lend a helping hand.

There have been historic periods when African Americans experienced support and encouragement from each other, such as Following emancipation from enslavement, when Juneteenth celebrations allowed African Americans to form communities, free from the constraints they had faced for hundreds of years. For generations, the laws of the land denied many African Americans the right to marry or to control of their children. They were not allowed to testify against White people in court. Emancipation and Constitutional extension of the rights of citizenship brought new opportunities. They could move about in search of work. They could seek out family members who had been sold to people who lived far off. They could forge new lives for themselves, establish new communities, and prosper where permitted.

Suggested Activity

When a mentor sets a grand table before you to help you develop yourself, stand up and help yourself. For it is inappropriate to say "No one cares about us. No one helps us."

About 50 years later, following the Armistice of World War I, African Americans around the nation gathered to celebrate their Veterans' heroic return from war abroad. At home, many found employment in cities that had been off limits before the war, breaking the debt peonage of tenant farming and the cycle of generational poverty. Many African Americans saw the benefits of supporting their own institutions and businesses, and rallied behind civic causes in clubs and organizations. The National Association for the Advancement of Colored Peoples and the United Negro Improvement Association flourished. More recently, African Americans lobbied for and achieved the declaration of the Rev. Martin Luther King, Jr. Day as a national holiday. African Americans have also supported and encouraged political officials from the grassroots level to the highest office in the land.

In communities large and small, African American churches, civic organizations, non-profit organizations, and political leaders continue a long tradition of reaching out to mentor and support Black teens. Take advantage of the opportunities to join these efforts.

WOFORO DUA PA A

"When you climb a good tree"

Be supportive.

Encouragement

Helping hands inspire good work.

COOPERATION
Build a sense of purpose and community with others.

The heart has thousands and thousands of muscle fibers. Its chambers fill and empty through a complex system of valves and paths. Electrochemical impulses fire the system, depending on the blood volume demanded from the heart by the body. The heart's internal cooperation is so essential that irregular heartbeats, racing pulses, and severe blood pressure problems can result without it. When the heart does not cooperate with itself, the body is in serious trouble.

Similarly, chaos occurs at specific levels of noncooperation in a society. This mass breakdown is accompanied by paranoia and extreme distrust. Frightful flights of women, the aged, and children to safer grounds; runs on banks; panic buying or selling; looting and riots, lynchings, and horrifying crimes are common when groups of people no longer experience internal cooperation. Families, neighborhoods, communities, cities, and larger areas can experience breakdowns in internal cooperation.

> ### Suggested Activity
>
> Examine the activities in your home that require internal cooperation among family members. What happens when you don't cooperate with others in your home?

Usually, outside help arrives to restore the order that is necessary for people to continue to live in the affected area. In neighborhoods, for instance, policemen are sent to homes where the internal disharmony has caused neighbors to worry about their own safety. The National Guard is sent to communities where internal strife has led to mass civil unrest and disobedience. United Nations peacekeeping forces patrol the streets in places where ethnic and religious conflict might escalate to massacres.

Our bodies have what we call an immune system. It knows the difference between what is "us" and what is "not-us"; what belongs inside, and what should not be inside. It protects us from diseases by recognizing and responding to cells and processes that we need to neutralize. Study the wisdom of your body. Begin to identify yourself as someone who has a concern with how your community and society functions. Put your hands in the dish.

WO NSA DA MU A

"If your hands are in the dish"

Recognize and repair signs of sickness in the community.

Participatory Government

Reach out to those in need.

PROPRIETY
Know yourself. —Socrates

Compromising your integrity is always distasteful. It may seem that compromise is required in some fashion all the time! It can be demanded in a trade-off for a job or a higher salary. It can be an inappropriate request from a stranger who somehow made you feel obligated to him or her. Or a "friend" might ask you to "help me drop a little something off" when all you wanted was a ride across town.

The thing to remember is that things change. You do not have to compromise your integrity to get what you want. Learn to recognize your mind's warning signal that you are about to be had. Learn to step back and reflect when you feel hesitant to go against your beliefs or values just because a peer is encouraging it. Learn to change your mind when necessary and to recover from a bad decision. Remember who you are and what you want in life.

Suggested Activity

Check out some books at your library that explain complex topics simply.

When I was about eight years old, I read the story of Pinocchio, the puppet. He was fashioned from a piece of wood by a carver named Gepetto, who so wanted a child. Pinocchio was unsatisfied, and went on a quest to become a little boy instead of a puppet. I wasn't aware of all the literary rules about character development and story line and suspension of belief. I was just fascinated by this little wooden figure that could talk and go on adventures and feel sad and want things that no one thought he should. Eventually, after many brushes with bad companions and scrapes with misfortune, Pinocchio becomes a little boy, much to the delight of Gepetto.

I think that as we develop throughout our childhood and teen-age years, we, like Pinocchio, encounter many missteps and misadventures on the search to become who we really are. Sometimes our desires and wishes entice us to try on all sorts of masks and outfits, much as we play dress-up. We watch rap videos. We play the parts. We imitate. Sometimes we do things we know are wrong. We compromise our integrity, mainly to impress others.

DENKYEM

"Crocodile"

The crocodile lives in water, but breaths air.

Prudence & Propriety

Good judgement fosters wisdom.

"Success is to be measured not so much by the position that one has reached in life as by the obstacles which he has overcome while trying to succeed."
—Booker T. Washington

"Impossible is not a fact. It's an opinion. Impossible is not a declaration. It's a dare. Impossible is potential. Impossible is temporary. Impossible is nothing."

— Muhammad Ali

Dr. William Conwill is a psychologist, healer, martial arts instructor, and university professor. He has served in a number of leadership roles in health, educational and governmental institutions. He is the winner of many awards, including UF Black Student Assembly 2008 Scholarship Award, AMCD Presidential Award for Meritorious Service and Exemplary Diversity Leadership Award, Florida Gold Coast Martial Arts Hall of Fame (Master Instructor) Inductee, Ringshout the Route National Rite of Initiation into African American Culture (Distinguished Elder), Arts of the Samurai Inochi Award, 2007 and numerous martial arts medals.

Many African American households have lost the presence of fathers, leaving many Black teens without that important male role model in the home. Projecting a model of a strong Black man, Dr. Conwill helps Black teens prepare to be adults in family, community and work. Calling on traditional African values embodied in Adinkra symbols, combined with a self-defense interpretation for each principle and a reading to help provide insight into themselves and their place in the world, Dr. Conwill offers keynote speeches and workshops for "Training Black Spirit" facilitators.

Contact info:
Harrison Conwill Associates
7819 S. Merrill Avenue
Chicago, IL 60649
mail@williamconwill.com

RONIN BOOKS FOR INDEPENDENT MINDS

CPSIA information can be obtained
at www.ICGtesting.com
Printed in the USA
FFOW04n0630260317
33880FF